GAME ON!

SONIC
THE HEDGEHOG

JESSICA RUSICK

**Checkerboard
Library**

An Imprint of Abdo Publishing
abdobooks.com

abdobooks.com

Published by Abdo Publishing, a division of ABDO, PO Box 398166, Minneapolis, Minnesota 55439. Copyright © 2022 by Abdo Consulting Group, Inc. International copyrights reserved in all countries. No part of this book may be reproduced in any form without written permission from the publisher. Checkerboard Library™ is a trademark and logo of Abdo Publishing.

Printed in the United States of America, North Mankato, Minnesota
052021
092021

Design: Aruna Rangarajan, Mighty Media, Inc.
Production: Mighty Media, Inc.
Editor: Rebecca Felix
Design Elements: Shutterstock Images
Cover Photograph: AntMan3001/Flickr
Interior Photographs: aaronmjr/Flickr, p. 13; AntMan3001/Flickr, pp. 21 (top), 23; ArcadeImages/Alamy, p. 19; Dave Monk/Flickr, p. 5; Evan-Amos/Wikimedia Commons, pp. 14, 28 (top); Everett Collection NYC, pp. 27, 29 (bottom); Fabio Santana/Flickr, p. 9; James D Case/Flickr, p. 20 (right); joe mama/Flickr, p. 15; John krizan/Flickr, pp. 24, 25; Manuel García Melgar/Flickr, pp. 11, 28; Manuel Sagra/Flickr, p. 17; Shutterstock Images, p. 21; Sonic Retro/Flickr, pp. 7, 29; Wikimedia Commons, p. 20

Library of Congress Control Number: 2020949740

Publisher's Cataloging-in-Publication Data
Names: Rusick, Jessica, author.
Title: Sonic the Hedgehog / by Jessica Rusick
Description: Minneapolis, Minnesota : Abdo Publishing, 2022 | Series: Game On! Includes online resources and index.
Identifiers: ISBN 9781532195815 (lib. bdg.) | ISBN 9781644945490 (pbk.) | ISBN 9781098216542 (ebook)
Subjects: LCSH: Video games--Juvenile literature. | Sonic Adventure (Game)--Juvenile literature. | Sonic the Hedgehog (Fictitious character)--Juvenile literature. | Sega Genesis video games--Juvenile literature. | Video games and children--Juvenile literature.
Classification: DDC 794.8--dc23

NOTE TO READERS

Video games that depict shooting or other violent acts should be subject to adult discretion and awareness that exposure to such acts may affect players' perceptions of violence in the real world.

CONTENTS

THE BLUE BLUR

A blue hedgehog in red-and-white shoes blazes down a hill, collecting golden rings as he runs. The hedgehog jumps to avoid spikes and bounces on top of an enemy robot. Then, he rolls into a tight ball as he races around a loop. Sonic is on the move!

Sega's *Sonic the Hedgehog* **franchise** is one of the best-selling video game series of all time. It has sold more than 140 million games! In 2020, there were more than 70 *Sonic* games. These included main franchise games and **spin-offs**, such as racing and puzzle games.

Fans love the *Sonic* series for its fun, speedy gameplay. Most of all, fans love Sonic himself. Since his **debut** in the 1990s, Sonic has remained a popular and recognizable video game character.

When Sonic first debuted in 1991, he was history's fastest moving video game character. Creators said Sonic's sneakers powered his super speed!

DESIGNING SONIC

In the 1980s and early 1990s, Japanese video game company Sega was competing with rival Japanese game company Nintendo. Over the years, both companies released **consoles** and games to win over gamers. This corporate battle became known as the "console wars."

In 1989, Sega released the Genesis console in the United States to compete with the Nintendo Entertainment System (NES). The Genesis was unsuccessful at first. Although the NES was four years old, it still outsold the Genesis that year.

The NES's games helped make it popular. Nintendo games featured well-known characters, such as Mario. Sega had characters, but none were very popular. Sega President Hayao Nakayama realized that to

RABBIT EARS

Another of Sega's early character concepts was a rabbit that could grab things with its ears. However, the ear-grabbing motion was too difficult for game developers to **program**.

Yuji Naka (*left*) and Naoto Ōshima (*right*) celebrate the twentieth anniversary of their creation, *Sonic the Hedgehog*.

compete with Nintendo, the company needed a character as recognizable as Mario.

Sega held a contest for company employees to submit new character designs. Submissions included a dog, a hedgehog, and an old man. Sega designer Naoto Ōshima and developer Yuji Naka considered these designs.

During this time, Ōshima traveled to New York City and showed the designs to passersby in Central Park. The United States was a large market for video games. Ōshima's research allowed him to learn what Americans thought of the designs.

Between the dog, the hedgehog, and the old man, the hedgehog was the most popular. When he returned to Japan, Ōshima shared his findings with Sega. He and other game designers liked the idea of a hedgehog curling into a ball to roll around and deal damage to enemies.

OLD MAN

Sega's "old man" character inspired the design of *Sonic the Hedgehog*'s villain, Dr. Ivo "Eggman" Robotnik.

The original Sonic character and game
cover in a book featuring Sega creations

Ōshima worked on the hedgehog's design. He gave it blue
fur to match the Sega company logo. At first, the hedgehog's
name was Mr. Needlemouse. But soon, the character got a new
name. Sonic the Hedgehog was born!

SONIC SUCCESS

In 1991, Sonic starred in *Sonic the Hedgehog* for the Genesis. The game was a **side-scrolling platformer**. It had multiple levels. The game's villain, Dr. Ivo "Eggman" Robotnik, had taken over an island to find items called Chaos Emeralds. As players moved through levels, they had to gather these emeralds. They also had to defeat Dr. Robotnik.

Like other platformers, players jumped to reach platforms, avoid obstacles, and take out enemies. But *Sonic* also focused on speed. Players sped through levels of loops and steep slopes. These features made Sonic go even faster.

Players also gathered rings. These allowed Sonic to absorb damage without losing a life. Special power-ups gave Sonic **invincibility**, superspeed, or a bubble shield.

NEW HEIGHTS

In 1993, Sonic became the first video game character featured as a balloon at the Macy's Thanksgiving Day Parade in New York City.

The Sega Genesis packaging featured an illustrated Sonic blasting across the box. A Sonic figurine stands beside the 1991 device and a toy TV depicting *Sonic the Hedgehog* gameplay.

Sonic the Hedgehog was a hit. Fans and critics enjoyed its speedy gameplay. Many even thought the game was more fun than Mario **platformers**!

Sonic helped Sega compete with Nintendo. During the 1991 holiday season, Genesis **consoles** outsold the new Super Nintendo Entertainment System. This was partially because the Genesis was sold with *Sonic the Hedgehog*!

Sonic's success led to 1992's *Sonic the Hedgehog 2*. The game **debuted** a fox character named Tails. In multiplayer **mode**, players could race Sonic and Tails head-to-head on a split screen.

In 1993, two *Sonic* TV cartoons aired. That year, Sonic was the most popular cartoon character among US boys ages 6 to 11. The *Sonic* **franchise** was booming!

Sonic the Hedgehog 3 debuted in 1994. It let two players control Sonic and Tails on the same screen. The game also introduced an **echidna** character named Knuckles. Both Tails and Knuckles would appear in future *Sonic* games.

SWIMMING SLIPUP

In *Sonic* games, Sonic can drown in water. This is because developer Yuji Naka believed hedgehogs cannot swim. In reality, hedgehogs are great swimmers!

In addition to *Sonic the Hedgehog 3*, the game *Sonic & Knuckles* also debuted in 1994.

SONIC SLOWDOWN

By the mid-1990s, Sonic had become as recognizable as Mario. Then the **franchise** hit a rough patch. In 1995, Sega released the Saturn **console**. That same year, Japanese electronics company Sony released the PlayStation. The PlayStation cost less and had more games than the Saturn. And the Saturn had been designed primarily for **2D** games. The new PlayStation was designed for more advanced **3D** games.

To compete with the PlayStation, Sega released *Sonic 3D Blast* for the Saturn in 1996. Despite its name, *Sonic 3D Blast* was not a true 3D game. Instead, it had an isometric, or angled, view. This

The Saturn

made the game appear to have a **3D** effect.

Fans were disappointed by *Sonic 3D Blast*'s **graphics**. They also disliked its gameplay. Instead of speeding through levels, players searched for and gathered birds called Flickies. Fans felt this was boring.

The Saturn **console** also fared poorly. By 1998, it had sold only 3 million units in the United States. The PlayStation had sold more than 11.5 million.

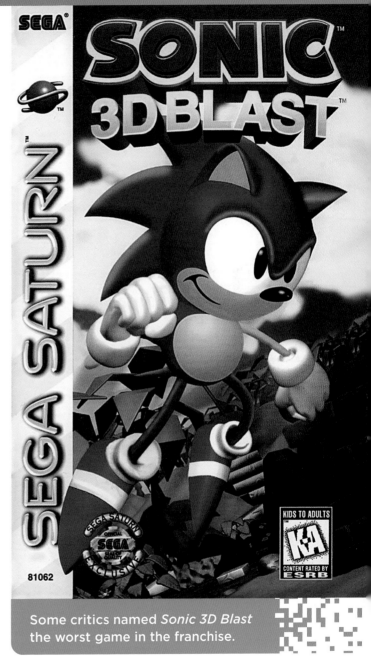

Some critics named *Sonic 3D Blast* the worst game in the franchise.

SONIC ADVENTURE

In 1999, Sega released a more powerful **console** in North America. It was called the Dreamcast. That same year, the first fully **3D** *Sonic* game, *Sonic Adventure*, **debuted**.

Sonic Adventure's gameplay was fast-paced. Sonic ran, rolled, and jumped through levels at speeds much faster than characters in other 3D games. Some critics pointed out **glitches** in *Sonic Adventure*'s gameplay. But most praised the game's **graphics** and speed.

Fans enjoyed the game too. By 2013, it sold more than 3 million copies, making it the most popular Dreamcast game ever. *Sonic Adventure 2* debuted in 2001 to similar success. Over the next 12 years, it sold nearly 3 million copies.

While the new *Sonic* games were popular, the Dreamcast was not. By 2001, it had sold just 3 million units in the United States. So that year, Sega stopped making consoles. Instead, it would focus on making games for non-Sega consoles.

In 2002, Sega released a *Sonic Adventure* game for its competitor! *Sonic Adventure 2: Battle* was made for Nintendo's GameCube console.

RETURNING TO ROOTS

In 2004, Sega released *Sonic Heroes* for the Nintendo GameCube, Microsoft Xbox, and Sony PlayStation 2 worldwide. The game featured many loops, corkscrews, and drops. Fans found these thrilling and **unpredictable**.

Sonic Heroes became the second best-selling *Sonic* game of all time. It sold just under 6 million copies over the next decade. But the **franchise** soon stumbled.

In 2006, Sega released *Sonic the Hedgehog*, which shared a name with the original game. But in this game, Sonic had to protect a human princess named Elise from Dr. Robotnik. The game had a darker tone that fans disliked. In addition, **glitches** made it difficult to play.

In the next years, the *Sonic* franchise worked to recover from its misstep.

OLYMPIC CROSSOVER

In 2007, Sonic appeared with former rival Mario in *Mario & Sonic at the Olympic Games* for the Nintendo Wii **console**. Players used the Wii's motion capture remote to control the characters as they competed in Olympic events.

00000150
00:26:59
O 015

In 2010, Sonic returned to his **side-scroller** roots in *Sonic the Hedgehog 4: Episode I*. The game featured **updated graphics** and redesigned levels. Many fans and critics felt this was a positive step for the series.

LEVEL UP!

Sonic Racing

Sonic has starred in several racing games. These games pit Sonic and friends against one another in fun-filled car races!

SONIC DRIFT

+ **Console**: Sega Game Gear

+ 4 playable characters

+ 18 tracks

+ 4 items, including Springs (allows players to bounce) and Red Boxes (allows players to temporarily speed up)

+ **Modes**: Free Run, Versus, Chaos GP

SONIC TEAM PRESENTS

SONIC DRIFT™

ソニック ドリフト

ゲームギア専用ソフト
GAME GEAR
1-2
SEGA

Many *Sonic* games were made for play on the handheld Sega Game Gear console.

2019

TEAM SONIC RACING

+ **Consoles**: Sony PlayStation 4, Microsoft Xbox One, Nintendo Switch

+ 15 playable characters

+ 21 tracks

+ 14 items, or Wisps, with different powers based on their colors; Ivory Lightning Wisp allows players to strike another player with lightning; Orange Red Burst Wisp allows players to leave trails of fire behind them

+ **Modes**: Online Multiplayer, Exhibition, Time Trial, and more

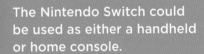

The Nintendo Switch could be used as either a handheld or home console.

7

SUPER SONIC

The *Sonic* series continued to bounce back. In 2011, Sega **debuted** *Sonic Generations* for the **franchise's** twentieth anniversary. The game featured levels based on earlier *Sonic* games.

In 2014, a Sonic TV series created a new generation of fans. *Sonic Boom* aired until 2017. The show was popular. But three games released to tie into the show did poorly. These were *Sonic Boom: Rise of Lyric*, *Sonic Boom: Shattered Crystal*, and *Sonic Boom: Fire & Ice*.

But *Sonic* didn't stay down for long. In 2016, *Sonic the Hedgehog* was **inducted** into the World Video Game Hall of Fame! The next year, Sega released *Sonic Mania* and *Sonic Forces*.

TWO-PART LEVELS

Each *Sonic Generations* level had two parts. The first portion was inspired by early *Sonic* **2D** games. The second was a **3D** portion inspired by modern *Sonic* games.

The trailer for *Sonic Forces* gave fans a glimpse of how the game allowed them to create playable avatars.

Sonic Mania was a **2D side-scroller** inspired by the original *Sonic* game. However, *Sonic Mania* had more detailed animation and new levels. *Sonic Forces* had both 2D and **3D** levels. In addition to playing as Sonic, players could also design their own playable **avatars**.

8

SOUNDS OF SONIC

Music is an important and beloved part of the *Sonic* **franchise**. Japanese **composer** Masato Nakamura wrote the original game's soundtrack. His **synthesizer** song for the game's Green Hill Zone level became especially well-known.

Elements of Nakamura's soundtrack have been a part of *Sonic* games since 1991. But each game brings new inspirations and collaborations.

Composer Tomoya Ohtani began working on *Sonic*'s sound in the early 2000s. He used music to highlight the games' features. For example, 2010's *Sonic Colors* was set in outer space. So, Ohtani gave the soundtrack an electronic, pop music feel. Other *Sonic* games have featured **orchestral** numbers and booming rap songs.

HELPING HAND

After *Sonic the Hedgehog*'s original release, Nakamura tried to play through the game to hear his songs. But Nakamura was only able to clear the first part of a level! So, he asked a friend to play through the game for him while he listened to his music.

A collection of soundtracks
from the *Sonic* franchise

9

RACING ON

The *Sonic* series continued to blaze ahead. In 2020, Sonic made his film **debut**! *Sonic the Hedgehog* was released in February of that year. A computer-generated Sonic shared the screen with real-life actors. The film made $57 million in US ticket sales during its opening weekend. This was a record for a film based on a video game.

Meanwhile, fans wondered what was next for the **franchise's** video games. In 2021, *Sonic* reached its thirtieth anniversary. Sega promised new games to celebrate.

Since its debut, the *Sonic* franchise has had its ups and downs. But Sonic has rolled, sped, and bounced back from every low!

RESEMBLE REDO

Film studio Paramount Pictures released a trailer for *Sonic the Hedgehog* in April 2019. Many fans thought Sonic looked too different from his video game counterpart. In response, Paramount spent months **updating** Sonic before releasing the film. Fans were happy to see a revised Sonic that looked more like the video game version!

Sonic in his 2020 film debut. Later that year, the sequel film *Sonic the Hedgehog 2* was announced for a 2022 release.

TIMELINE

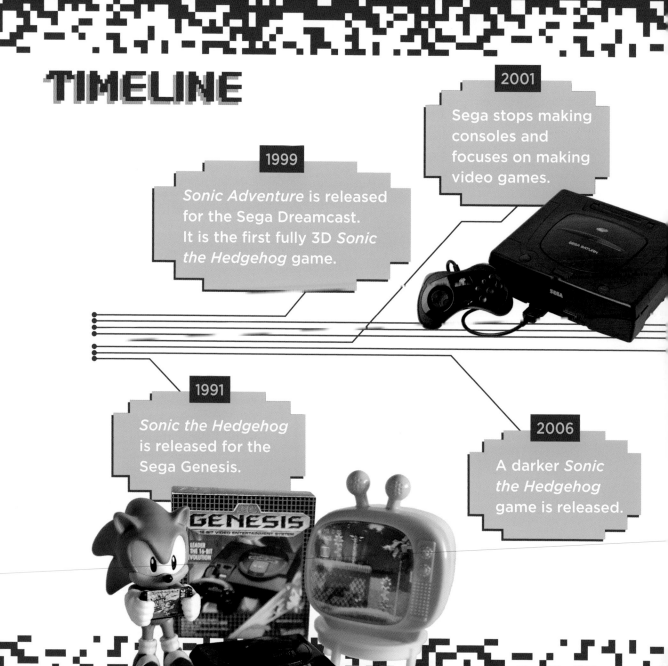

2001

Sega stops making consoles and focuses on making video games.

1999

Sonic Adventure is released for the Sega Dreamcast. It is the first fully 3D *Sonic the Hedgehog* game.

1991

Sonic the Hedgehog is released for the Sega Genesis.

2006

A darker *Sonic the Hedgehog* game is released.

2011

Sonic Generations debuts for the franchise's twentieth anniversary.

2017

Sonic Mania and *Sonic Forces* are released.

2020

A Sonic the Hedgehog movie is released in theaters.

2016

Sonic the Hedgehog is inducted into the World Video Game Hall of Fame.

GLOSSARY

avatar—an icon or figure representing a player in video games.

composer—a person who writes music.

console—an electronic system used to play video games.

debut (DAY-byoo)—to first appear. A first appearance is a debut.

echidna—a toothless, burrowing mammal with a spiny coat.

franchise—a series of related works, such as movies or video games, that feature the same characters.

glitch—a minor malfunction.

graphics—images on the screen of a computer, TV, or other device.

induct—to admit as a member.

invincibility—the quality of being too powerful or capable to be conquered.

mode—a way of operating or using a system.

orchestral—written for a large instrumental music ensemble, called an orchestra, to play.

platformer—a video game in which the player-controlled character moves and jumps across platforms of varying heights while avoiding obstacles.

program—to write computer software.

side-scroller—a video game in which the action is viewed from the side as the player-controlled character moves across the screen, usually from left to right.

spin-off—something that imitates or is inspired by an earlier work or product.

synthesizer—a usually computerized electronic device used to produce and control sound in making music.

3D—having length, width, and depth, or appearing to have these dimensions. *3D* stands for "three-dimensional."

2D—having length and width, but lacking the appearance of depth. *2D* stands for "two-dimensional."

unpredictable—unable to be guessed or declared in advance.

update—to make something more modern or up-to-date. An update is a more modern or up-to-date form of something.

ONLINE RESOURCES

Booklinks
NONFICTION NETWORK
FREE! ONLINE NONFICTION RESOURCES

To learn more about *Sonic the Hedgehog*, please visit **abdobooklinks.com** or scan this QR code. These links are routinely monitored and updated to provide the most current information available.

INDEX